Botanical Wall Art For T

MW00899181

WELCOME TO THE FLOWER, FERN & FRUIT DECOR BOOK

First of all, thank-you for your purchase. This book is designed for those who wish to decorate their home with beautiful botanical art. Inside you will find ready to frame art which was made by some of the masters of botanical illustration, it has been hand curated to find the best examples of botanical art.

All of the art in the book has been hand restored by myself, by carefully removing yellowed pages, restoring colors, linework and removing blemishes which had built up over time. These beautiful artworks can now be enjoyed in the way that their original artists intended.

I hope that you enjoy displaying them in your home!

I really value your feedback, so if you find anything that you think can be improved please let me know (tim.stowes@gmail.com). I can then make the next edition even better for all botanical art admirers!

How To Use This Book

Each botanical print is on a page on its own. Once removed from the book each page measures 8 by 11 inches, this allows the prints to be easily placed in a 8 x 10 inch frame. It also gives a 0.5" space on the top and bottom of the print so that you have a little more room if you need it, depending on the frame you wish to use.

Before removing a print from the book, open the book wide on the page that you would like to remove. If required, bend the spine of the book back so that it allows the book to lay flat in front of you. This will help to make it easier to remove the page when it comes to trimming.

Simply remove the page that you require by carefully cutting down the dotted trim line which is maked on the left of each print.

Once the page has been removed, it can be placed in a frame, or if you are using a larger frame a mat can be added around it.

The Prints

THE 46 PRINTS IN THIS BOOK ARE ARRANGED AS FOLLOWS:

The first group of 29 images are of flowers.

The next group is 3 cacti prints.

Following that there are 10 fern prints.

Finally, the last 4 are fruits.

Printed by: Createspace

ISBN-13: 978-1722022358

ISBN-10: 1722022353

First Printing, 2018

Manufactured by Amazon.ca
Bolton, ON